All Just

DAVID HERD is a poet, critic and teacher. His recent essays on poetry and politics have appeared in *Almost Island*, *Parallax* and *PN Review*. He lives in Kent.

Also by David Herd from Carcanet Press

Mandelson! Mandelson! A Memoir

DAVID HERD

All Just

CARCANET

First published in Great Britain in 2012 by

Carcanet Press Limited
Alliance House
Cross Street
Manchester M2 7AQ

www.carcanet.co.uk

A CIP catalogue record for this book is available from the British Library

ISBN 978 1 84777 163 6

The publisher acknowledges financial assistance from Arts Council England

Typeset by XL Publishing Services, Tiverton
Printed and bound in England by SRP Ltd, Exeter

for Alpha

Contents

The thought of our time finds itself confronted
with the structure of the exception
in every area.

Giorgio Agamben

3 a.m.

At three in the morning, Rimbaud wrote,
The candle grows pale,
All the birds cry out at once
In the trees: it's over.
The sky seized [le ciel s'est chargé]
Already the staccato,
Buy bread.

He must have worked all night.
What he imagined was a vanishing point,
A tenacious correspondence between diverse spheres.

Or rather, a kind of serenity [eue'maneria, beautiful day]
The new politics which remains largely to be invented.

That's what it's about,
3 a.m.
Candle. Birds. Trees. Bread.
Seized [s'est chargé],
Already the staccato.
Just about, merely
Circulating.

Sans papiers

Quite different from those who stayed at home
Many of whom developed with them
As they spread – gambling, choosing where to invest
Based on conflict in an empty land,
There to make substantial voyages –
A few, scattering, made their way across;
Through cold, similarly barren landscapes
Mitigated by panic – birds, deer –
The first of them, helped by sudden strange warmings
In small bands, though many must have starved;
Till they could go again, ranged against the chilly edges
Where parts of the message must have disappeared
With time but also through violence, errors in transmission
So it couldn't be framed how much movement there had been;
Only to advance, similarly toward resources
Outward into the wood-belts as knowledge itself moved
With them as they spread, gambling forwards
Given curiously into deep unease.

To the historians – a letter

Maybe there was a place here.

High enough to issue a warning, the question, always,
                                    was how to get at it
Whether the approach came from land or as the records indicate
                                    'seawards'
In the event compromised how to cut the fortifications off.
This is how it was imagined.
And so Twiss, seeing the problem, called for a Grand Shaft
The new barracks not sixty yards over high water mark
But to communicate with them a mile, and over
Footpaths so steep and chalky 'a number of accidents
                                    will unavoidably occur'
Especially after floods. 'I am therefore induced to recommend
                                    the construction
Of a shaft the chief objective of which is the convenience
                                    and safety of the troops,'
And he was no engineer but the fix was obvious,
In the outer a triple staircase, the inner acting so as to form a well
With windows cut in to illuminate, so they could picture in the dark
Afford, in the event compromised, a secure retreat.
So he saw it, the Redoubt, a solid island
Cut into the hillside the trenches revetted (faced)
                                    with brickwork
Like a barricade, from to clothe again, 're' and 'vêtire'
Directed inwards in accord with conventional wisdom,
The imaginary variously augmented as deemed necessary by
                                    the Royal Commission
To add caponiers, being covered passages across a ditch
                                    around a fort,
Literally 'capon enclosure', from the Spanish, 'caponera',
Later a bridge the inner section fixed by a pivot
Swung into a recess of which the outline is still discerned
From recessus, recedere, to go back
In the event the fortifications to be totally cut off.
Thus the imaginary, a series of strong points connected by
                                    ditches

And though the approach never came a limit was set;
That Twiss saw to, built into the conception, dry moats (the lines)
At all times the possibility of controlled withdrawal,
Which nobody would call a place only a state in time of
                                        turbulence,
Suspension, from the Latin, turba, crowd,
The bridge that swings into a dedicated recess
As deemed necessary shutting the whole situation down.
But check this, the day construction was completed the war
                                was almost over,
This, the approach they anticipated never came
Not landwards nor seawards,
That the imaginary cuts deep
This historian, 'therefore
Off limits'.

Outwith

I –

Shabbier than usual
Not much whereabouts
Put a call in,
'Meet me wouldn't you
This evening by the trees,'
Where the road hangs and the river
Ruptures to become mountains
And the camp you built
Out of packing cases
Stands in.

'And if you beat me to it
Come up with some names wouldn't you
Whatever settles you as comfortable.
Send me a picture.'
I have this photograph
Waiting for you with my phone
Some tree in winter
Articulated by an office building.
Not much.
Nowhere really.

On not being a man who is Piero della Francesca

1

Where we live among has not the mood of Arezzo
No, girlfriend, these are not the church steps
And girlfriend, in this interior no painter on commission
Lent himself to the manufacture of a morning light;
So making it a 'perfect example' [Kenneth Clark, *Civilization*],
Girlfriend, where we live among is not that
Nor in governance, girlfriend, where we let the space and these
Are not the steps, and believe it, girlfriend,
Whatever else we hope for now it will not be grace –
Even though among us we have an idea
Distributed casually across particulars
Boys, for instance, drinking coffee along the sea wall –
But that is not a step, this is not a church, there is no interior,
Where we live girlfriend complicit moving equally among.

2

Or not the mood, or *not* the manufacture,
Distributed casually through the morning light
Across particulars, boys for instance, drinking coffee
Whatever else a perfect example beside the church steps;
Only believe it, girlfriend, we have an idea
Between us in governance, distributed
Where we live among across commissioned space
Casually through the interior which is not now a church
Making it, in particulars, a manufactured grace –
Which sets us, girlfriend, among where we live,
Light, if we like it that way, along the steps,
Drinking coffee among the boys along the sea wall –
Only, girlfriend, you are not a painter and there is no commission,
Girlfriend where we step complicit equally among.

And so, girlfriend, we have an idea, even here where we live among
A perfect example whatever else beside the church steps
Of governance distributed casually across boys in particular
Trying to make it, girlfriend, among the manufactures of a morning light;
An idea with the mood of a commission
To live in governance across the interior
Distribute the particulars of a manufactured space
Which is a step, girlfriend, setting out from where we live, here
Where we know, taken casually across the morning in the name of grace –
Here even where we know,
Sat with the boys among particulars
Drinking coffee across the morning beside the sea wall –
Where we catch the light and we sit on the steps and, casually, girlfriend,
Set out among particulars we know equally moving complicit.

On not being a man who is Piero (out set)

Or

                morning

Across

                    steps;

Lent

              distributed

          commissioned space

Casually

      particulars

             among

    along

     for instance   boys

    step

             complicit.

And Piero, a further word

When Piero della Francesca painted
The Church of St Francis in Arezzo
Under governance of Florence
Legend of the True Cross
Serene ·
Conflicted
'The most perfect morning light in all the Renaissance'
In the name of intelligence
He constructed
A complex emotion.

Song of the road

On the road towards the tenement
Clothed heavily
Not long gone since
A man stops.

'Boubekar.' 'Boubakar.'
This is a function of the imagery.
In the darkness surrounds us
He tells his own story.

Poem beginning with a phrase from Whitman

Until that which comes –
what? –
has hidden evenings?
has sat up watching as the earth curves
carrying the boats away, absconded,
which has ridden roughshod,
gathered momentum crossing furiously over marked space
settled, temporarily, on the outskirts of a shanty quarter,
which was uncertain,
had not habit of fathoming
how deep to bury in,
which walked the boards,
figured longing,
followed the curvature of necessity,
which dwelt among the implications of a fastened room,
stipulated English,
which travelled through shifting environments,
mountains dropped savagely into agricultural terrain,
crossed at speed,
lay down cramped among the cargo,
listened watchfully as the decision got made,
elsewhere unrecorded,
lips unstruck,
until that which comes
'from vigorous practice',
'long trial',
loosens the dialect,
'a system of calls and warnings' among us,
among us we settle
in a dark place.

Song of the cigarette

Girl among girls
one of those
repeated sequences
fag end of summer
tide gone
into evening becoming evening allover
inherited vocabulary
mouth on her
starting
plumready

For a friend, after a translation

The morning is glamorous.
In the flush Kent sky
Birds with mouths to feed
Splenetic with song.
And you, friend, at the station
Big with news,
Trashy in the poppy orchards –
Great expectations.

3 notes towards a love song

1

The world is feral today and still
There is much between us
This dumb old November weather
Consequential, nothing but itself.
The land before us so thickly clothed already,
This is objectively a love song,
Standing us opposite
Densely manufactured
By slow degree.

2

Feral, like a love song.
The shy old planet has nothing to say to us this morning.
Dumb,
Consequential,
Manufactured old
Earth.

Nothing to say –
Maybe we should get on with it,
Objectively, a love song,
Allow things,
Comrade,
To be difficult between us.

3

Camarade, this morning,
Things have this shy way of happening,
So that if we should speak
It is barely established
Either one of us belongs

In this weather we have
Making all things difficult
So that even your being here is a blessing
In these several senses which pass into each other
Showing in the circumstances
What the world might hold.

Establishing
There is much between us
As dumb old November plays itself out
And we stand opposite contemplating the distance
By some slow degree,
Forage quietly in each other's language
Manufacturing a love song

Objectively,
Comrade,
Among trees.

Fact

This is just to say —

when a detainee

from the Dover Immigration Removal Centre

applies for bail,

if he has a bail hearing —

which he is not entitled to attend —

though his lawyer is,

and the Judge is,

and a representative of the Home Office is —

the bail hearing —

imagine —

is officially un-

recorded.

Song of the mobile

Some young guy
sunshinewarmenough
time in his pockets
phone rich
minute by minute
conscious and volitional
clean
shaven
heavybored

3 poems becoming elegy

1

This back pocket's for keepsakes,
An invitation to an exhibition,
Items to remember and maybe one day use.
Or discard,
Structures pass,
All structures pass,
The clear cut of an October morning carries a heavy moon.

Which we'll see again
Notwithstanding all the indicators.
It is ultimately elegy underwrites the poem.
Shatters it.
Structures pass.
Assemblies of people.
The poem choosing bashfully
Here among.

2

And as the dream of every cell
is to become two cells,
so what·the poem hankers after
is another poem,
splitting itself off,
feeding on the residue,
among stones,
among structures untouched

where the elegy lies
where the poem handles circumstance
caught among the fibres of the old guy's clothes,
the hats he wore great hats,
the thought is difficult,
cell by cell,
October among.

Lately it has become apparent
that the nation is deserving elegy.

There are practices among us
we are tending to forget.

For which the elegy works because the poem is here among
modelling its behaviour on things which pass.

Codes, counteractions,
the poem has its lists.

The disorientation of the citizen
detained without charge.

Not, actually,
understanding where he is.

Vulnerable, isolate.
Things pass.

You among

When the plums were first ready
before the first one fell
when the roses were not yet planted
and the ground was dry,

before the eucalyptus was cut down
bent double beside the gate
before the sea surged
before the value in the market dropped,

as the mallow came through
not for the first time
beside the road helped
by a brief warming,

as copies proliferated
as the clematis bloomed
as people arrived
to complete a hazardous crossing,

as the errors accumulated
before the apples ripened,
before the news broke, before the panic
before the denial stopped,

in dense populations
among prosperous economies
when the plums were first ready
but before the first one fell

before the goldfinches had gone,
before the nets were dry
before the crisis was with us
before a big old moon

as you walked from the table
to the kitchen door
we were glad that night
to have you among us.

Ecology

Along the broken road
nearby the disparate houses
where summers, coming into purple
the mallow blooms,
scattered,
carting children,
complex tools and fishing nets,
women,
'environment acting',
stop and exchange;
beneath wires where
afternoons
goldfinches gather,
'Adoration of the Child and the Young St John',
nearby the outbuildings,
a variant,
slipped open early,
'based on conflict',
as morning comes;
where seagulls stand
allover into language,
where mallow blooms purple along the broken road,
scattered, disparate,
'beautifully economical',
you stood one time
struggling
to arrive at terms.

Ecology (out set)

What stands discrete

scattered against the outbuildings

mallow   goldfinch   complex terms

and you, stood there

not knowing if you're coming or going

'beautifully economical'

'hostile world'

Bric-a-brac

After that day
barely thought worth recording in natural history,
since the moment
the order of expectation stopped –
since the
inquiries,
after –
some people inquire after –
whose absence –
the day the conversation broke off –

Since then –
bric-a-brac –
plums lain smashed among the mallow –
putting it all together,
one by one –
the road,
the lilac tree,
these facts are of plain signification –
and all the time wanting
to tell you about it.

Where things stand

1

Where things stand is

as the starlings congregate

as the conflict escalates

as the children come back

worldwise, allover the place

curiously given

handing over the receiver

you call it   through

2

Where things stand is:

intensification of information
product placement
allover the place,
complex routes

'the "dream" …
of every cell:
to become two cells'

some woman
standing up to it all
for everyone's sakes

One by one

The poem splits,
It has no desire to become a nation,
It traffics in meanings, roots among stones,
Mallow,
People,
The things they have with them,
Corrugated outbuildings
Along the broken road.

Immigrant through the streets
It craves sources of stability,
Processes it might settle its elegy among;
It splits,
To begin again,
It seeks the moon broken across the estuary,
People arriving,
One by one.

Song of the sea

Underneath the crane
where the land stops
sea becoming
safe
in a yellow hard hat
some kind of seventies moustache,

graven
by the weather
the man is building a monument,
level after level
just such
here.

Song of the passing truck

1

Watch the young girl rise.
She is very worried.
Think of it as speaking
To somebody else.

Think of it as speaking
As a truck goes past.
Hair knotted. Beautiful
As any wild rock pigeon.

2

As watched –

As outward any
Wild rock pigeon –

She knots with moss roses
As since only
She resists –

Beautiful therefore –

Speaking –
In the natural economy –

Watch –
She speaks beautifully

As the trucks go past.

Simon's bag

We're in the Place de la Comédie –
Some – where the trams –
Some – keep on coming
Past Victor Louis' Grand Théâtre
Backs on to Place de Jean Jaurès
Where people park cars hardly
Thinking about Jacques Brel
The album before he died
People thinking pockets
Les Marquises
People thinking exit only
'De la Réalité du Monde Sensible'.
And cops. People thinking cops
Swing by on blades past
Citizens pushing strollers considered
Good cops largely
Largely bad cops
Drop down on to Rue Esprit des Lois
Outside the shadow of les Girondins
Falls across the park some
Somewhere where the trams go
Steeled loose people
Thinking bag colour most
Moderate deputies of the Revolution.
Thinking maybe blue maybe different bag
Some book on the table
Too big for anybody's pocket
Thinking sunglasses Hôtel Regent
Grand Hôtel de Bordeaux
Brel paying tribute to Jaurès
Talking about Bergson
Articulating lived time
In people standing
Still and walking steps from the theatre
Down among the trams.
And some. Down among and some
Nearby where the station

The streets needed widening
Boulevards comparable to Haussmann
All kinds of everything articulated through.
Sky. Check. From the pavement up.
People thinking skateboarders carrying secrets
Back to work and
Chocolate malted
Simon's book
Right bag.

Objective song

When I was younger I wanted things
fixed. I sat and
        watched the traffic
        waiting for
        the vehicles
        to slow.
        The factory
        stayed open all night
        set about
        the neighbourhood's
        business. From
        where I watched
        there were things
        it was imperative
        to know.

It has taken a while, I don't suppose that
factory stayed open
        long after I
        don't know for certain
        the people
        who made those things
        only now
        as the cars go past
        and they put up
        those buildings up
        everywhere
        I notice
        objectively
        the boat's
        unhinged.

Some woman pressed

There is an urgency in relief tests the language
taxes the manufacturer whose medium is sound
generates between fabric and emphatic particular
a tension of election difficult to emulate in words.

So it can be said. There is an urgency in relief,
the manufacturer in language testing sound,
finds between fabric and elective particular,
a struggle of emphasis difficult to emulate in words.

Or escalate, where sounding is all the medium
the struggle towards particular difficult to apply
except in tension, moments of election,
crisis in the fabric generating urgency in words;

Manufacturing in language a sculptor's drive towards particular
junk maybe, some woman sifting, sorting through rags,
picking things out, generating urgency in language
emphasis in a medium whose total fabric is sound.

Where relief is difficult to emulate, the sculptor's drive towards particular
emphasis struggling out of fabric where the medium is words,
sifting, sorting through rags, generating tension among us
difficulty in language where the test is sound.

And where the sculptor has the medium of relief, driving out of the material
twisting into particularity, difficult to emulate in sound
on a broken road a woman sifting, sorting the tension among us
escalating an urgency difficult to manufacture in words.

Which the sculptor generates as relief, a drive into urgency
twisting the fabric into particularity emulating material claim
manufacturing struggle, dignity of emphasis, on a road
some woman sifted, pressed into sound.

Some woman pressed (out set)

On an unadopted road
dense with potholes
thick with the insistence
of a collared dove
a woman
heavy set
not from the immediate neighbourhood
sifts
sorts through
the tension among us

To a friend, after a word by Charles Olson

When the plums lie smashed
at the end of the garden
we have a recognition

the season's slipped

seventy —
that would have been something

a tone is set

bright, against the houses
October song

The hearing

I –

Don't know if there is a poem here.
With all the beautiful things you
We walk down by the river
In the cold through the Africa rooms of the British Museum
As Leo Frobenius saw it you
Tell a story of the half-brother who rose up –
I have never seen you angry
I have never seen you drunk.
I have seen you with the waitress
Listened as you ask after my family
Pictured you on the beach waiting for the agencies to show
As the boats come in oblivious to place
Each time asking a different question you saying,
'Ceux qui restent sont-ils pas mes amis.'

I –

Have slept while you dance waited
As the season approaches as the
Dogwood flakes and you show up late since
You are always late or I am
Caught in traffic people
And cars in between us texting
'I should soon be with you
My life has registered its charge.'
Listened as you refused to go mad
Settled to a study of happiness
In the room you occupy uncluttered by belongings
Only a rucksack full of books
Taken down as guides as you make your way across
Showing us the route we carved out for ourselves and you,
'Maintenant je suis maudit, j'ai horreur de la patrie.'

I –

Have sat at the back of the court watched
As proceedings go unrecorded as the
Season approaches and you say 'guarded'
And your translator reports 'protects' suffering
No qualification as the man from the Home Office
Tells your story, 'Was it Dr Kumara
Who helped you leave your country
Or as you subsequently reported Mr Souma?'
Waited as the questioning persists wondered
What the implications sound to you as the
Dogwood flakes outside a courtroom
And nobody present thinks to ask if you were scared
Sans papiers pitched forward into shadow
Condamnée pour jamais a l'oubli de tous,
You saying, 'Mister David it's all happening again.'

Song of the ultimatum

As the woman on the phone
'stability exactly adjusted'
cigarette in one hand
suede boots,
holds out, for a moment –
some kind of purple tunic arrangement –
'still, deep rooted'
an ultimatum exists.

Somehow it seems

Quietly through the streets,
we carry ourselves
circumspect, complicated
by anxiety, scenting fear
inherited with the debt,
honest-to-goodness geopolitical
adventuring, blow back
against the trade winds
settling its covenant
here. Leaving us much to learn
about not belonging,
about edging ourselves cautiously
through unfamiliar streets,
not knowing the signs,
Aries the ram
though the currency is stable
Orion the hunter
Gemini the twins,
presiding over buildings
of indeterminate provenance
barely specified conscious always
the franchise might change,
alter, enhance the demand:
slate we recognise,
some version of sandstone,
London brick.
Even though as drivers
we know when to slow
which comes as basic now
in automobile technology
still there are practices
among us we're learning
not to use; this is blow back
we follow it on the wind,
the finest clause
in the closest small print,
covenanted, guaranteed

maturity, by some antique
name. Leaving us edgy
difficult to disclose,
unless by some woman maybe
who just came through,
carrying a baby,
on false documentation,
drawn by the language
because the syntax runs deep,
uncertain of her surroundings save
this is probably Dover,
subject to requirement
manoeuvred by the state
though she has a function
maybe with some people
maybe in some doctor's home,
to be shadowed forth
establishing a structural equivalence
contingent, understanding
she doesn't belong
frightened, not following the terms
some woman
witness among us,
no one,
this is Dover,
let her drive the car.

Song of the stewards

Couple in the bus shelter
not much happening
seagullsallover
fashionable shoes
wise stewards
not so
interested in the timetable
that's their story
political life cannot

Show and tell

Let's say we did but didn't like to
Where does that leave us,
Deeply woven, establishing a living,
Scraping the surface of unconsecrated ground,
Making a home and all that,
Setting out the particulars,
Always on the verge of some kind of landscape,
Struggling to convince ourselves the way we wandered
How it mattered finally what enclosure is.
There maybe, and say we didn't like to object
For so many good kinds of reason
Because this was summer and at the periphery there was patching
                                     to be done,
Holding the whole thing down on a broadly show and tell basis,
Whatever it was yesterday we stumbled into
Chicken wire, gum paper, items we had forgotten it was possible
                                         to lose,
And which mattered as materials building up a picture between us,
Of us in our competence stretching hungrily for the phone,
Because we'd ordered out and like it or not
The man from the restaurant always delivered a fortune cookie,
One for each of the signatories:
'Every day a good day',
'You've got nothing to lose'.
Which does stack up because we are what we know after all,
A piece of work creating rubble some other will one day use,
Picking over the top, putting some kind of house together even
                                 where it most abounds,
Stringing out a washing line over by the horizon some woman
                                 steps to in her husband's shoes;
Tugging at the threads, the fundamental direction of travel,
Densely woven into the geology the moment the seasons turned,
Forgetting only that the curve runs both ways
Because after all the recession of particulars is stubbornly deceptive,
Because looking at it among the patchwork you'd hardly notice
                                 she was there.
But say we did and didn't like to,

Say perhaps we were busy drinking coffee,
Outwith a passage deep in the imagery identifying the source,
Scrambling the contours
Leaving latitude the only option,
Say she showed up,
Say she was refused permission,
Say she was incarcerated the moment she tried to leave.
Just say, here,
Among the particulars,
Blown back amid the complexity of unknown laws,
Trying to pick up the threads and all that
Always on the verge, barely thought worth recording,
Leaving us quietly the way cookie tells it due process.

Song of the breath

Boy in the bed
long day afterward
grazed by expenditure
breathing
clear,
knees, half-bent
still
sweethairbefalling
turned sideways
frail construction

We do this, we do that

What it's about is 6 a.m.
Awake since dawn and the evidence of bird song
Sirens fixing the drift and so objectively speaking
Something happening,
News that stays noise,
All just.

It's what we should pitch I think,
'Evidence of bird song',
The habeas corpus of just wandering about
What happens   happening
Before our very eyes.
My 6.
Woke early
Listened to the sirens just.

At five I went down to buy some bread
The work men are on the move everywhere,
I went to bed when the sun
Was bringing the woodlice out from under the tiles
What's always enraptured me here is the morning
In summer and the December evenings,
I have a pretty room over a courtyard
With no far end to it.

My 4 even.
I listen to the birds seized
By the sound of some kind of emergency,
What it has to be about is 6 a.m.,
That the custodian present proof,
That you have the body
Pitching uncertainly,
All   just.

Some details maybe

Some details maybe.
This gentle pressure we are under
Like this was a fable in which indignation
Was a forgotten move
And you party politely
On Saturday nights unable
To contemplate oblivion
In case the adjudicator with the keys to your pocket
Announces the bridgehead down.

I have looked across that bridge.
I have noticed several details:
Stars, animals, the savage journey across the plains,
Europe laid out like a map.
I think tonight of all nights you should party
Build a canopy out of nothing
Till tomorrow
We'll rage.

A footnote to the American Constitution

Or set about it this way, Taney could see no pretext
that the authority the constitution has confided
under any circumstances be usurped
at its discretion the people of the United States
but every citizen hold life at the pleasure
in whose district he happens to be found.
Sited.

No matter.

In a short session

a bill to provide indemnity for suspension of the writ
to remove Taney's objection that Congress
not the President had the power
passed December 8 Senate finally cleared.
So establishing the basis

for all

subsequent application

couching:

the day the beach filled
though the season was already through
nobody sure   could be
they'd get another chance
only the sun was out
so this was a good day for beer
camped   whole families hardly shopping
not thinking whereabouts
in the sun to be sure.

Thinking maybe lunch maybe
which   way children
down beside the water headed
each way dunewards
people thinking Amstel maybe
since the   day looked long enough
barely anybody present at it
compelled to move
anybody   laid out before the sun

people thinking Kronenberg even
whole families playing soccer
sure   to be before whom any such
persons acting plainly
given only time.

This much I can report.
I didn't speak to the sun directly
minded he was busy and
anyway since he talked to O'Hara
the principle of constitution
seemed hardly to have changed,
though this was Camber Sands
nobody's version of Long Island
such commons in the present
by the authority understood
that he shall   people talking Polish
people talking bodies the way the wind picks up

making it creditable   and warm
like an avenue in springtime
or some such
some kind of whereabouts
this much I'm ready to report:
one, looking out for the first time
people at the water thinking sure enough,
that day definitely   Taney's objection applied.

Deportment

When you say

    after this

        so hot day we're having

June 2nd

    2010

        a woman said

that sun

    has got his

        hat off

I check you.

    On.

        Hat.

On.

'Oh,' you say

    'so, on a

        day

like today

    lovely

        to walk in

you say the sun's

    hat

        is on.'

'It's from a song.'

'A song?'

The sun has

got his hat on.

June 2nd

Two thousand ten.

And so the sun

goes on.

Song of the cart

When an old woman
carting her shopping
makes her way home
along the broken road
in her trainers it's a struggle
centralised, homuncular
dwindling resources
redandwhite
dress

They offered me a television. I offered them a phone.

Not to become angry we tread carefully
Around the truth the kind of
Day you've had the kind of
Weather you who register the world
Not stacking up
Though you don't ask much
Only that some things
Might not yet happen
As you hang on
As sometimes on the phone
I tell you my day
You tell me yours

Not angry, modern,
Since none of the places you go to
Stand open on the territory
And none of the symbols you carry
In the pocket of your rucksack
Settle your whereabouts as you
Walk along the shore
Unfixed, uncertain what might happen
Only that difficult things
Will come to pass
And so you say nothing and
None the wiser
I say nothing in return.

Some might call it shopping

Or isn't the truth
We dropped everything to have that Coke
Not much whereabouts to speak of
No such August afternoon
Though it was the city
That much we could name
And this was a way we'd come
To articulate happiness
Call it improvising on the evidence
Needs be.

And truth be told what we need surely
Is a new kind of document equal
To the places we constructed between us
Where the road hangs and the river
Drops below the stones so we can
Know it at least as witness
Adequately call it.   Phrase the affect
To have, to hold, the Habeas
Corpus of just stepping out, hanging
At the side of the track a mark
Of everything we've done together
Persons   present according
After names keep.

Four poems by way of document

1

Standing out and sometimes
miles from any place
likewise carrying an alias
following the direction of the land
as it distances to some degree
making the manner of the way
an issue, limited in any case
according to the long delays,
made either better or sometimes
true according to the present
jurisdiction, whether a person
copies or whether a person
acts, not so tender now
but plainly marked
taking the view in from
where it matters where
he stands same as any body
making out   said order.

2

By standing

                any one of them

In cause of this   that

Where the miles go
Where the persons

Brought   enacted

Who were present
After the party

What the distances shall bring

Making it   whatsoever

Out by commons

              assembled

3

Which is what matters
Stànding in this sàme place
Where the days appear
As part of the process
And there is no necessity
To pretend each one
Making it so plainly expressed
Standing like an act
Like a person present
Sometimes sure   sometimes
Likewise limited
Standing still and waiting
As the commons shifts.

Or say it this way
There is no felony in presence
Not in standing plainly
Making out the distance
Such commons assembled
Bringing persons into place
That this be the process
No necessity to attest
Each one making it   the way
The city shifts   carrying
Each one notwithstanding
No one to witness
No offence.

4

having marked the land

to assemble a city

standing watching

by commons out

Letter to the Corinthians

Maybe
We should elect
To practise
Love's
Criteria

Love shan't ask
Reckoning only
There's some backstory
He could tell.

If he chose to
One afternoon
As the snow arrives
In Lewisham.
'We are become …'
In borrowed Reeboks
Chinos
'… offscouring'.

Fugue

Nearly everything is unchosen.

This dark morning as the lights line up against the train track
the seagull has no obligation to exist
first battling with then gliding in the direction of the wire,
headed south,
a northerly,
though it has a right to;
against a blocky sky
harsh and morning eventful,
blown back before dropping into its specific course,
no sound except to sea,
only the gulls awake early enough –
writing with a torch on so as not to disturb the light.

Unchosen
lies at the root,
cold, limited –
the wind is harsh and maybe we can venture 'unforgiving',
as witness gulls,
deeply subjected,
it is a dark place six months of the year
northerly
north to south,
and there are few safe harbours.
Few to choose
and anyway it is a common enough reversal,
the ancient covenant is in pieces,
lifted and then blown back,
tossed about,
such are the forces,
something like 'the definitive abandonment' –
indifferent,
southerly,
Dover is one of them. Stop.

Living creatures are strange objects –
are they not.
Even at this hour the light is discouraging,
telephone wires rock endlessly at the back of the house
establishing the need,
gulls
all the way down to the structure of protein
battle up,
hold their own a moment,
arc back under through the breeze –
in face of strict restriction,
physical and ideational,
dark six months,
neither destiny nor duty written down.
It was not to be the last case of its kind of course
there are plenty recorded in history,
nearly everything is unchosen –
in the torchlight writing a bit,
making a note to write.

Because the theme runs deep –
the morning isn't glamorous
beneath the bruise becoming visible is a cloud-slate grey
and nearly everything
cold,
arbitrary, unpredictable,
evidence surely of the strangeness of their condition.
Which is a political reality,
evidence surely of a political reality,
like a gypsy living on the boundary of an alien world –
ragged maybe,
irregular,
fairly adventurous,
quietly adapting in the half light. Stop.

Dover is the limit –
is it not.
Let's set the limit objectively now, shall we,
as by analogy this morning

the wind blows south
forcing the seagulls
inland
hawking their whereabouts early enough,
fugue-like,
objectively –
a man from Guinea Conakry. Stop.
Like a fugue,
objectively,
unique and irrefutable witness,
tumbling,
co-ordinated –
a man from Indonesia. Stop.
Designated 'fugal', in flight,
decked with the certainties of science,
upon which they opened their eyes –
a man from India. Stopped.
Beaten and detained
following the common trajectory,
emulating the curve
drifting northward
imagining the map,
laid out in way stations,
inward with the land
from which he emerged
only arbitrarily,
intimate with the limitations of a biological being,
like a fugue,
fugue-like,
wintering darkly
passing sometimes
crossing,
watching the shipping home,
taken with a view,
vulnerable,
physical,
ideational
bones
nerves
a man from Eritrea. Stopped.

Stop.

Up the hill
Nearly everything is unchosen.
Most of the lights are off.
All over seagulls.
A person steps out from his van.

You'd hardly know it,
not even for looking,
not even if a person were looking –
from the French,
or from the Italian,
from the Latin,
fuga.

Fuga –
steps out.
It is possible to specify colours,
object among objects,
a collared dove.

Everything nearly,
France.
Dover France.

Fuga –
unchosen.

Stands.
Stand.

Document

The population was largely composed of Guarani Indians, and the section of the great family in these latitudes had from the earliest days been noted for its easy-going qualities.

The old man began to sing
in the cracked voice of old age.

Hello

I am Paz Marcuzzi.

Acknowledgements

Some of these poems, sometimes in different versions, appeared in the following journals: *Mascara*, *Otoliths* and *PN Review*. My thanks to the editors: Michelle Cahill, Mark Young and Michael Schmidt.

The poems 'Outwith', 'They offered me a television. I offered them a phone' and 'Some might call it shopping', were written as one half of a collaborative exchange with Sarah Vap and published in *Like Starlings*. Thanks to Sarah, and to David Hawkins for the commission.

Thanks also to Steve Collis and Jay Millar for the BookThug chapbook *Outwith*, in which some of the poems in this book appear.